SOUTH AFRICA'S WILDLIFE HERITAGE

SOUTH AFRICA'S
WILDLIFE HERITAGE

ANTHONY BANNISTER & PETER JOHNSON
TEXT: BY MIKE NICOL

CENTRAL NEWS AGENCY (PTY) LTD
CNA BUILDING, LAUB STREET,
NEW CENTRE, JOHANNESBURG 2001

Reg. No.: 01/02033/06

FIRST EDITION 1980
SECOND IMPRESSION 1981
THIRD IMPRESSION 1984
FOURTH IMPRESSION 1985
FIFTH IMPRESSION 1987

COPYRIGHT© PHOTOGRAPHS: ANTHONY BANNISTER AND
PETER JOHNSON 1980
COPYRIGHT© TEXT: MIKE NICOL

PHOTOSET BY McMANUS BROS (PTY) LTD, CAPE TOWN
LITHOGRAPHIC REPRODUCTION BY UNIFOTO (PTY) LTD, CAPE TOWN
PRINTED AND BOUND BY LEEFUNG-ASCO PRINTERS LTD, HONGKONG

ISBN 0 620 07278 4

CONTENTS

ACKNOWLEDGEMENTS

Anthony Bannister and Peter Johnson would like to thank the many people and organisations whose assistance made this book possible. They would particularly like to mention the following (the order of listing in no way reflecting the help of any one as being lesser than that of another) and apologise for any omissions:

The Director, Park Wardens, Officers and the many other members of staff of the National Parks Board of South Africa; the Director and staff of the Natal Parks Board; the Director and staff of the Percy Fitzpatrick Institute of African Ornithology; Jon and Sally Panos and all the staff of the Gametrackers and Safariplan organisations; our wives Barbara and Claire; our children Andrew and Sue Bannister and Susan Johnson; Maudanne Bannister; Dr Cecily Niven; Patrick and Marina Niven; Anthony and Ginny Johnson; Joan Lawrenson; Tim Longdon; Sir Hugh and Lady Beadle; Julian Ogilvie Thompson; Isak Barnard; John and David Varty; Rod and Coleen Patterson; Adolph and Liz Waidelich; Les Mamashela; Bruno Lamoral; Rudi van Aarde; the many pilots who have flown us so competently in light aircraft and helicopters; the Division of Nature Conservation of the Transvaal Provincial Administration; The Wildlife Society of Southern Africa; the Nikon and Hasselblad camera companies; and not least our designer, Walther Votteler, for his sensitivity, skill and imagination.

INTRODUCTION

On hot days nothing moves in the bush. The horizon is a watery haze and even the fish eagle retires to his perch in a dead tree to let the still hours pass. At the water's edge three turtles lie like worn black stones.

But as the sun passes its zenith in the afternoon, the bush slowly comes back to life. Through the straggly trees a herd of impala moves hesitant and twitching towards the water. Warthog break cover and trot down to a favourite mud wallow, and the fish eagle, its challenging call cutting through the sounds of the awakening bush, launches out over the pan.

Tiny kingfishers drop again and again like spangled jewels after insects. Sternly wading the shallows, a hamerkop keeps its own counsel, while a crocodile floats lethally still in the water.

The impala warily leave the grass and start out across the bare no-man's land that surrounds so many waterholes. Each muscle tensed, ready to flee at the hint of danger, they walk gingerly to drink. They take their fill and head back to the safety of the bush. Suddenly lion strike.

A lioness charges the impala and one, perhaps a little slower than the rest, breaks from the herd and races away into the open. The ambush works and a second lioness attacks the panicking animal, lunging onto its back and quickly snapping its neck. The rest of the herd bound off a short distance and then relax and begin to graze; for the moment they are safe.

Such is the elemental simplicity of life in the wild where the dead return nutrients to the earth which in turn will green to feed the living through another thousand years and more.

As our world becomes more urbanised, as great cities spread out and what was not so long ago vast tracts of wild land become real estate, as factories belch and farmers clear new land to feed the hungry world, so the imperative to get away, to regain a sense of one's place in the grand design grows ever stronger. Perhaps it is this need that brings more and more people to the wilds where life is revealed at its most fundamental.

Africa more than any other continent still offers vast areas of wilderness teeming with animal life. And nowhere within one country in Africa can you experience such a variety of wildlife as in South Africa where you can go from the humid forests of the Pafuri region of the Kruger National Park where there are still great herds of elephants, to the wintry snow-covered Drakensberg where the mountain zebra pick their way along the precipices; to the harsh deserts of the arid west coast that bloom in spring with so many species of daisy that botanists have not counted them all.

South Africa's amazing variety of fauna came to exist through this enormous range of habitats – the forests and marshes, the mountains and coast, and, most prolific of all, the many and varied grasslands which once extended from the Transvaal southwards to the Karoo.

For the natural habitat is the all important key that ensures that wildlife survives. A habitat is to all intents and purposes a home. It is the area born of the encounter of the four elements – earth, fire, air and water – which forms the backdrop for the interaction and evolution of insects, reptiles, birds and mammals.

When the habitat changes, be it for man-made or natural reasons, the living things within that habitat must adapt, move on, or die. Take the early Karoo, home to South Africa's first prehistoric forms of wildlife.

The Karoo has a fascinating history dating back some 280 million years. In those days rain fell continuously, and the land was covered with vleis and swamps. Then, gradually, world temperatures began to drop, so that they were almost constantly below freezing point and the great glacial period had begun. Enormous ice masses embedded with mud and rocks ploughed across what is now the Karoo, scouring deep grooves in the mother rock. These ancient grooves have now been exposed through erosion, and debris carried by the ice from areas hundreds of kilometres away lies scattered on the Karoo plains. This period, known as the Dwyka glacial period, lasted for hundreds of thousands of years.

But gradually the thaw began. A rich plant life took hold in the Karoo Basin, and although there are relatively few fossil finds from this time, fish remains and the earliest reptile found in South Africa – a swimming reptile – have been uncovered.

In the more temperate era that followed (the Ecca period), the ice disappeared and mountains such as the Swartberg range in the south of the Karoo formed. Life became more various and more numerous in the swamps and with temperatures still rising, the Karoo became home to the most interesting variety of creatures ever to live there.

In this era known as the Beaufort period, mammal-like reptiles that were mostly herbivores, developed. Both fish and invertebrate remains have been found from this period but they are far less renowned than the reptilian fossils of the Ecca period. New forces were at work here however. The climate was still warming up, the rain had become less frequent, the water-table as a result had lowered considerably and massive lava flows had begun to move over the land.

For some strange reason this period is not nearly as rich in fossils as the Ecca period, but several forms of dinosaur date from this time. Although dinosaur remains are rare their footprints were left pressed into mud which later became layers of sandstone. Some dinosaurs were lightly built, walked on two legs and were in some respects like the modern ostrich. Others were massive, measuring up to six metres long and walking on all fours.

It was out of this prehistoric, marshy landscape that the Karoo grasslands of three hundred years ago and more, evolved. Today, many parts of the Karoo are semi-desert, but there was a time within the history of white settlement in the country, when these plains were alive with herds of game; herds the size of which it is impossible to conceive today. And such scenes were not confined just to the Karoo, they could be seen all over the country.

Man's impact up to this point was minimal. He had hunted with bone or stone weapons and he had hunted only for food. He had no greater status in the order of things than any other predator and his hard existence provided little chance of a sudden population boom which would place great burdens on the land. But a new factor emerged to disturb the ancient order. The black man with his iron implements, his cattle and his crops moved down from the north. His cattle and his fields began to displace and disperse the game, and his presence began to impinge on the freedoms of the Bushman and Hottentot who had lived in the subcontinent for so long.

Still later, white men with their guns, cattle and crops began moving in from the south. Man was now not only vieing for the grasslands with the

wildlife herds, but man competed with man for room in which to live, to feed himself and his livestock, and, in the dryness of the subcontinent, for water. The farmer changed the habitat by tilling the soil, and also sought to protect his cattle from predators. So began a tragic saga which saw some animals driven to extinction before the end of the nineteenth century and left many other species precariously on the brink.

The decimation was piecemeal and few could begin to realise what was happening when the first antelope fell to gunshot at the Cape in 1652 – a new tradition of slaughter was begun. Within 30 years the large mammals, including the elephant, rhino and hippo, were extinct on the Cape Peninsula and hunters had to journey to the Hottentot Holland Mountains to find game.

But wholesale slaughter began only when the gentlemen-hunters of Europe crossed the mountains of the Cape and came upon the vast herds of the Karoo.

Hunter-naturalist Sir William Cornwallis Harris describes how in December 1836 he came across a large herd of blesbok on a Karoo salt pan. 'Never having killed any of these antelope, and our stock of provisions requiring to be recruited, I mounted . . . and never heeding whither I sped, dashed into the thick of them. Dealing death around, I continued to scour the plain, the herd before me increasing from hundreds to thousands and reinforcements still pouring in from all directions when crying "Hold enough," I stayed my hand from slaughter.'

His actions were typical of the hunters and farmers of the times and little could he begin to perceive that with herds so plentiful they could ever be destroyed.

Explorer Gordon Cummings was awoken one morning by the noise of springbok and got up to have a look. He writes: 'I beheld the ground to the northwards of my camp actually covered with a dense living mass of springbok, marching slowly and steadily along, extending from an opening in a long range of hills on the west through which they continued pouring, like the flood of some great river, to a ridge about a mile to the north-east over which they disappeared. The breadth of the ground they covered might have been somewhere about half a mile. I stood upon the fore chest of my wagon for nearly two hours, lost in wonder at the novel and wonderful scene which was passing before me, and had some difficulty in convincing myself that it was reality . . . During this time their vast legions continued streaming through the neck in the hills in one unbroken compact phalanx.'

The plunge to extinction by several species was swift. In Swellendam in 1791 a hunter put his rifle to his shoulder, squinted down the sights at a velvety blue antelope and pulled the trigger. The impact spun the buck around and it collapsed – the last blue buck had died. This magnificent animal, said to be a relative of the sable antelope, according to the hunters of the time, had a bluish lustre which faded immediately after death.

Some 60 years later the Cape lion, larger and more splendid than the African lion, with a rich golden coat and more luxuriant mane was extinct too. Then in August 1883 a quagga died on the cold stone museum floor of the Koninklijk Zoölogisch Genootschap in Amsterdam. As this rather oddly-marked animal, similar in size to a zebra but with stripes only on its neck and head, had been a great attraction at the zoo, they wrote asking for another one. But there were no more. The quagga, too, was extinct.

Specimens of these three species, all unique to South Africa, can be seen only in natural history museums in Britain and Europe.

At the start of the twentieth century, the eleventh hour had been reached for many species of wild animal. The bontebok – an antelope unique to the Cape – was down to about 300, and there were probably no more than 100 mountain zebra left. But the trend for these two creatures at least, was not irreversible for in the sanctuary of specially proclaimed parks and reserves, neither is endangered any longer.

One of the most exciting conservation stories of the century concerns the great white rhinoceros. Rhino had fallen to hunters' guns primarily because of its horn. Many people believe that powdered and consumed, the horn restores a man's sexual vigour. (While this is completely untrue, the myth continues and today rhino horn has become an increasingly costly item.)

In the 1930s it was estimated that there were no more than 38 white rhinos left in South Africa. This remnant population lived between the Black and the White Umfolozi rivers, and their survival there was largely because the area was riddled with tsetse fly which effectively kept both man and cattle out with the twin menace of sleeping sickness and nagana. Alarmed, some far-seeing conservationists and the Natal Parks Board began the long process of nursing the white rhino numbers back to a healthy state in the Umfolozi wildlife reserve.

In 1963, Operation Rhino took on a further dimension with the help of the drug M99 which allowed the animals to be immobilised and translocated to other reserves. Today there are about 2 000 white rhino in South Africa and specimens have been sent to zoological gardens and reserves all over the world.

This conservation of the white rhino secured the survival of the animal in the whole of Africa, not only at its southern end. In the last decade alone, East Africa had lost 90% of its remaining rhino population and Kenya then imported white rhino from South Africa.

Work by the Natal Parks Board has also secured the survival of the black rhino which numbers a meagre 480 at present. This rhino roamed throughout South Africa and Namibia except on the Highveld and in the arid Kalahari regions. Yet, by the 19th century it had been exterminated over most of its southern African range. It became extinct in the Free State in 1842, the last Cape Province rhino was shot near Addo in 1853, and about a century later they were extinct in the Transvaal. Only in Natal did a small population survive – in the Umfolozi, Hluhluwe and Mkuzi Game Reserves – but even these numbered a mere 100 in 1930. Concerted efforts led to the present population being gradually built up and the animal was reintroduced to the Addo Elephant National Park and to the Kruger National Park.

Unfortunately South Africa still has many mammals, birds, reptiles and plants on the endangered list. The main reason for this is that their habitats have been so markedly altered by man that they can no longer survive. Conserving wildlife in a country such as South Africa where old traditions and attitudes die hard, is extremely difficult. The frontier spirit still burns strongly in many people and is reflected in extremely aggressive attitudes towards predators and scavengers.

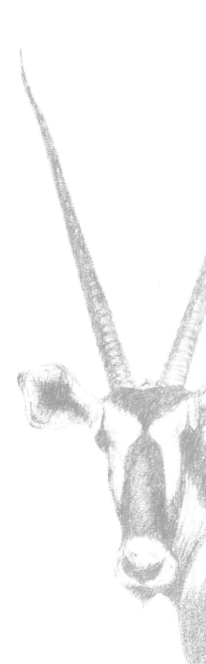

To the farmer, cheetah or wild dog are still vermin against which he must protect his cattle. Many eagles, too, are regarded as pests when they are actually of benefit to the farmer. Were it not for the crowned eagles of the Knysna forest, for example, there would be a boom in the dassie population and farmers would suffer.

A dead crocodile elicits no sympathy. Yet crocodiles control the number of barbel in rivers and this in turn allows the more nutritious species of fish to thrive.

Not many people like wild dogs. They are branded as wasteful killers and farmers will shoot them on sight. Not surprisingly there are probably not more than 500 left in the whole of South Africa and there is a very real possibility that they will die out. Yet these along with all predators are essential in controlling wildlife populations and because they prey on the weak and ailing, only the strongest survive to breed.

The scavengers, particularly hyaena, jackal and vultures, are another group of animals universally despised. Few people however, stop to consider what the veld would look like if it were not for these creatures. Imagine if for a few months no one carted away domestic refuse; very soon cities and suburbs would be ravaged by plague and disease. Without the scavengers, the same would happen to the veld.

Obviously the best way to ensure the survival of wildlife and natural areas is to create reserves and parks. Although South Africa became aware fairly early of the need to conserve her natural heritage, the area set aside is little more than 3% of the entire country and only two of the parks, the Kruger and the Kalahari Gemsbok, come up to the 100 000 ha laid down as an internationally acceptable standard.

In certain areas such as mountain ranges, South Africa has taken effective measures to preserve the natural habitat but possibly the most exciting project of the future is in the Karoo. Some 20 000 ha have already been proclaimed near Beaufort West, but this could be merely a cornerstone of a park that stretches westward to the Atlantic coast and southeast to the Plains of Camdeboo.

Apart from walking trails there would be wagon trails, following in the ruts of the early settlers. Even the little country towns could be incorporated, for many have hardly changed over the years.

Wilderness trails have become increasingly popular in the various parks and reserves. These trails give people the rare opportunity of seeing the creatures of the African bush in their natural environment.

Because most wildlife sanctuaries are so small they require careful management. One cannot merely fence off a small section of land, trap animals inside it and then expect it to function as if all nature's checks and balances were in action. Without being able to migrate, the number of browsers and grazers would soon build up to the extent that they would gradually strip the trees and grass exposing the earth to the forces of erosion. It is frightening how quickly a formerly lush reserve can be reduced to a lifeless wasteland. Frequently this necessitates that animals be culled within these very areas set aside for their protection and it is this aspect of management that is unacceptable to many. When the press gives broad coverage to an international effort to save the rhino from extinction, how can one explain the necessity to cull them in the local reserve? How can specimens be sold to private game ranchers who then operate hunting safaris to shoot them? How can wild animals be translocated to other countries when about 5% of every shipment will die? How can scientists catch dolphins and imprison them in pools for research purposes? These emotion-charged questions perpetually bedevil management.

Obviously no management techniques can work unless managers know what they are dealing with and here scientific research is vital. The scientific study of animals where it entails killing specimens or subjecting them to traumatic tests will always be a controversial issue. In the days of the naturalist, Burchell, it was necessary to kill animals in order to learn more about them. Today immobilizing drugs keep the animal alive while it is being examined. It must be acknowledged that the more man can learn about his fellow creatures, the better the position he will be in to protect and conserve them.

It is of fundamental importance, for instance, that the 'carrying capacity' of any given area be determined. By 'carrying capacity' we mean the number and type of animal that would be able to exist in a region of a given size without destroying the habitat. This is why elephant and buffalo have to be culled in the Kruger National Park each year. One must not lose sight of the fact that the Kruger Park cannot be maintained for elephant alone; it was created to sustain a wide variety of species and man must sometimes step in to keep the balance. So when elephant populations overstep the carrying capacity, some are culled.

The culling of elephant, or any wildlife for that matter, is a highly scientific operation and as humane as possible. Furthermore, every part of the culled animal is fully utilised and the revenue gained in this way used to further benefit the reserves.

South Africa is a country with a long seaboard and therefore has many and varied coastal habitats to conserve as well. The importance of these is often overlooked both from a wildlife and a commercial point of view. Few natural areas are less capable of withstanding the onslaught of human pressure. Many of South Africa's estuaries, which are the nursing grounds of the country's fish resources, need urgent protection from pollution, excessive and insensitive development.

These days economic considerations make wildlife conservation an attractive industry for immense revenue is brought in by tourists. On a more emotional level some argue that wild animals have a right to live and we must respect that right. But there are even more important reasons. For instance because all domestic crops and animals were originally wild, it is possible that in some dark time in the future we may need to draw afresh from the natural habitats we have preserved. In the past wild animals have been of use to man in medical research and this trend continues. The only creature other than man which contracts leprosy is the armadillo and experiments on this animal led to great benefits to humanity. Many plants contain complex chemicals used in medicines but which are difficult to manufacture in synthetic form, and many more have qualities yet to be discovered.

What this all adds up to is that wildlife conservation concerns human survival. Without natural habitats there would not be the broad genetic base that evolution must draw on if it is to continue. In other words, if we do not conserve, we are closing the door to future options.

THE LOWVELD

Some call it the Bushveld, some the Lowveld, others know it only as the home of South Africa's greatest wildlife sanctuary, the Kruger National Park. This is the north-eastern Transvaal where the Pafuri and Levubu, the Letaba and the Sand rivers flow turgid-brown into the Limpopo.

At six o'clock on a summer morning the sun is already a scorching disc low in the sky. The bush ticks quietly with life, and in a fragrant tambotie a crested hornbill flops heavily from branch to branch. On a sandbank in the Levubu a crocodile grins snaggle-toothed in the sun while unseen in the river's murk a lone Zambezi shark hunts 400 kilometres upstream from the sea.

This is the Pafuri region of the Kruger National Park – an area of giant baobabs, wild tumbled gorges and rich woodland. Of all the Transvaal Lowveld this northern region is the wildest and richest. All the large African mammals can be found here and in the several fine private game reserves which hug the boundaries of the Kruger National Park.

For centuries the mosquito and tsetse fly were natural custodians of this land, the diseases carried in their bite deterring man from disturbing the natural order, and today it remains among the most splendid wildlife areas anywhere in Africa.

A cheetah (1) snarls, and the distinctive black line from eye to mouth lends graceful symmetry to its compact features.

In 1912 Colonel James Stevenson-Hamilton, Kruger Park's first warden, counted a mere 25 elephant in the region. The great herds had been made gun-shy by ivory hunters and, what was left of their numbers had crossed to Mozambique. Over the years, however, in the sanctuary of the Park the elephant has taken up residence once more and multiplied so that there are some 7 500 today. This herd (*previous page*) with trunks uplifted sniffing for danger, huddles about the matriarch – a wise old cow who during her lifespan of 60 years or so has learnt much of the ways of the wilds.

At birth an elephant calf weighs over 100 kilograms and when fully grown a bull can attain 6,5 tons. To maintain this huge bulk, the elephant spends much of its day feeding – consuming vast amounts (3). These feeding habits have made culling a necessary means of keeping elephant populations within bounds and at the same time limiting the devastating changes they cause to the habitat – particularly when their numbers are high.

Pouring litres of water down its throat, a hefty elephant (4) shows off its fine tusks. To help keep its temperature down in the tropical heat, its massive ears are supplied with a rich network of blood vessels and as the elephant flaps its ears, so its blood cools before returning to the body.

For the game watcher, nothing is as certainly rewarding as a day spent quietly at a waterhole.

Never far from water, and most usually seen browsing riverine vegetation, is the waterbuck (5). This somewhat shaggy antelope is easily recognisable by its distinctive white marked hindquarters which, as someone aptly remarked, look as if the waterbuck had sat on a newly-painted lavatory.

African legend has it that the waterbuck has an odour which acts as a crocodile repellent. One could almost believe this to be true judging from the nonchalance with which it has been seen to wade belly-deep into crocodile infested waters. Park rangers who have witnessed crocodile attacks on waterbuck say that crocodile will attack waterbuck with the same alacrity they will any unwary antelope. However, when chased by lion or wild dog, waterbuck instinctively plunge into water where their enemies may hesitate to follow.

The waterbuck is one of several species of antelope which hide their young. For two to four weeks after birth, the tiny waterbuck calf remains concealed in tall grass or undergrowth, remaining motionless at the approach of danger and visited by its mother only to suckle. For the rest of the time the mother makes a point of ignoring her offspring for fear of attracting predators.

Slaking its thirst at the waterhole is the most vulnerable act for any antelope. These impala (6) drink with every muscle tensed, ready for instant flight at the hint of danger. But predators take advantage of this brief interlude when the antelopes' heads are lowered, and the patient observer at a waterhole may well be rewarded with a kill.

Impala are by far the most numerous antelope in the Kruger National Park, and they fill the same niche as the springbok in drier parts of South Africa and the Thomson's gazelle in East Africa. As the most numerous antelope, they are also the most preyed upon and in a sense act as a buffer between the predators and the other antelope species. There are some 53 500 impala in the Kruger National Park and their numbers continue to swell, thanks to the favourable rainfall in recent years in the woodland savannah where they live.

No two zebra have the same stripes (7); however, when the animals are on the move the visual confusion of the blizzard of lines may serve to blur the individual outline within the herd, making it more difficult for lion – the zebra's chief enemy – to mark its prey.

Unlike the mountain zebra, Burchell's or the common zebra has stripes that extend to the belly. Highly sociable, they form herds not only of their own kind but often in association with wildebeest – the zebra's superior eyesight combining with the wildebeest's excellent sense of smell to make for more efficient predator warning.

Perhaps the ugliest visitor to the waterhole is the warthog (8), trotting about, tail held comically upright like an antenna as soon as the creature breaks into a run or is disturbed. The comparison is not altogether inappropriate, for in tall grass, family parties or sounders of warthog are visible to one another only by the tips of their tails. No doubt this serves to signal alarm as well as the whereabouts of the members of the sounder.

At night the warthog generally retires to a burrow – usually someone else's that he has expropriated and made his own by lining it with grass. Favourite living quarters are those of aardvarks which feed at night when the warthog rests up.

6

7

8

Diminutive dweller of the dense bush in hot areas such as the Pafuri region of the northern Kruger National Park, the suni or Livingstone's antelope (9) is seldom seen for it is a shy creature. This female probably weighs less than eight kilograms. The large gland visible beneath her eye exudes a strong musky scent which is very noticeable in areas where this little antelope makes its home.

Common to the Pafuri region of the Kruger National Park is the aristocratic sable antelope (10, 11) with its magnificent curved horns, black satin-sleek coat and contrasting white underbelly and facial markings.

Sir William Cornwallis Harris, the famous hunter, was the first white man to describe this superb beast. It was pointed out to him some 130 years ago by his bearers in the Magaliesberg Mountains not far from present-day Pretoria. It is probable that the sable antelope never lived south of these mountains and certainly the herds of 100-strong reported then, are a thing of the past. Little more than 1 500 inhabit the Kruger National Park today.

Unlike the kudu which will retreat from danger rather than fight a predator, the sable antelope with its powerful armoury of horn, lacks nothing in fearlessness and will even face off lion. Under attack, the male will go down on its knees, scything with his horns and putting even the most aggressive lion to flight. Foolhardy predators charging an angry sable antelope have been known to impale themselves.

Some 400 species of bird grace the Kruger National Park, but the black korhaan (12) seen giving its characteristic raucous cry is not found here. However, an extremely common bird is the yellow-billed hornbill (13), shown eating the caterpillar of an African moonmoth. Most hornbills seal their wife and young into the hollow of a tree, leaving a hole just big enough to poke food through. Only when the nestlings are old enough to fly, do the parents break down the wall. Standing out like a tiny brilliant blue jewel against the vegetation, a malachite kingfisher (14) watches for flying insects. On its massive and untidy nest in a thorn tree, an African hawk eagle surveys its domain (15).

13

14

15

Scourge of many birds' nests is the common African egg-eater (16). This little snake lives almost exclusively on birds' eggs and an adult, which has a head and neck hardly thicker than a man's finger, can swallow a fowl's egg without any difficulty. To hunt, the egg-eater slithers through trees and shrubs sniffing for a tasty morsel with its delicate forked tongue. Sometimes the parent bird succeeds in chasing the snake away but it is only a brief reprieve for the reptile returns to claim its meal as soon as the bird leaves the nest to feed.

This egg-eater is in the process of swallowing a dove's egg. To do so it forces its head downwards and over the egg, the skin of the jaw and neck stretching almost unbelievably as the egg slips through the mouth and into the throat. The snake then closes its mouth and a special row of teeth, which are actually inward projections of the spine, crack the shell and the egg collapses. The snake waits about five minutes while it swallows the yolk and then regurgitates the collapsed empty eggshell.

In the broad natural order, the egg-eater should not be seen in negative terms for it, too, has a place and a positive function. Not only does it help keep bird populations within limits – but in the case of birds such as quelea which damage farmers' crops, it can have a beneficial effect.

South Africa has only one member of the bovines or oxlike animals and that is the Cape buffalo (*following page*), massed here with horns creating a solid defence and nostrils flared to catch the scent of danger. Both their sight and hearing are poor yet these animals, except when old, ailing, or young and careless, are not often preyed upon. These heavy-set animals with their massive bossed horns have a reputation among hunters for savagery if wounded, but left in peace they are in fact placid animals.

The buffalo has a fascinating role in the functioning of the ecosystem for this hefty animal tramples the tall coarse grasses as it grazes and browses. Such grasses are often un-suitable for other antelope and when the tender new shoots come up afresh after the trampling, several species of antelope are able to feed on the new growth.

Like cattle, buffalo need to drink daily and therefore rarely stray far from water. Although they were once common throughout the country, they are now confined to the Addo National Park in the Cape, to the Natal wildlife reserves and to the Lowveld. At the turn of the century the buffalo was almost extinct in the Kruger National Park, victim of rinderpest and the rifle, and at the time there were thought to be no more than 20. However, the current numbers stand at about 29 000 and culling has become necessary.

Lion (18) are probably the greatest single attraction of the Kruger National Park and indeed of all the Lowveld wildlife reserves.

They tend to hunt by night, preferring to spend the day resting in the shade and then rousing to the hunt only when driven by hunger. Here a cub sprawls nonchalantly over its mother. The spots on the youngster's fluffy coat will disappear as it grows older – it is possible that they are the remains of camouflage carried by forest-dwelling ancestors.

Initially cubs introduce a certain harmony to the pride and the lionesses share the task of caring for them, but even so, many do not survive to adulthood for until they are about 18 months old they are not competent hunters and they feature lowest in the pecking order at the kill. As time passes, the gentle indulgence towards them in their early youth is replaced by increasing aggression from the adults.

Neither particularly swift nor energetic, lion are often outrun by their prey and as many as four out of five hunts end in failure. Once the victim is down (*following page*), the entire pride arrives to claim its share and the lionesses who usually are the hunters must hold back while the males take their fill. Next the lionesses feed and, lastly, the cubs – who must wait their turn or else accept sharp rebuke.

By day the spotted hyaena (19) can be seen skulking close to a kill waiting for the lions to move off so that it can lumber in to help clean up the remains. Although scavenging is generally despised in our value system, it is a vital function of the veld for creatures such as the hyaena, marabou, vulture and even the lowly maggot hasten the return of nutrients contained in the carcass back to the earth.

Unlike lion, wild dog (20) allow their pups to feed first. The adults sit back and keep off any would-be scavengers while their young tuck in. Adults will then return to the pups too young to have joined them on the hunt and regurgitate meat for them to eat. On the hunt, the pack hunts as one, generally running down its prey over several kilometres and then tearing it apart without the nicety of a *coup de grâce*.

Another animal that scavenges for scraps is the black-backed jackal (22), although it also hunts in its own right for birds, rodents and other small mammals.

The much-maligned spotted hyaena (23, 24) is not the cowardly animal as so popularly portrayed; this animal is the ultimate opportunist scavenger and, in terms of survival, a most successful creature. If he can scavenge, he will, but at night the hyaena pack joins for the hunt. After running down their prey they make short work of the carcass, for the hyaena has the most powerful jaws and teeth of any African carnivore – even grinding up the bones so that its droppings are white with calcium.

The Lowveld has more insect species than anywhere else in South Africa. Seen in global terms this is not surprising, for insects can claim to be the most successful form of life on this planet; they are found in every corner of the world and in any given area constitute 80% of all animal life.

One of Africa's largest insects is the emperor dragonfly (25) which hunts flying insects, often far from water.

Because it cannot fly, the toad grasshopper (26) must rely on his fine camouflage to keep him out of trouble.

A far more beautiful creature is the tiger moth (27) which begins life as a brown and hairy caterpillar which even most birds will not eat.

Often seen building its distinctive mud nests on walls, the mud wasp (28) is a devoted parent for it stocks the nest with paralysed jumping spiders so that its young will have a continuous supply of fresh food.

A beautiful peacock butterfly (29) suns itself, wings open, in the early morning.

In October the wood stork (30) arrives in South Africa from the north. It is usually found near water and on flood plains, stalking on long legs through the shallows, often with head submerged, its long beak probing out aquatic insects, crabs, fish, frogs and small mammals.

Suspended in their thousands from the roof of a cave, Egyptian fruit bats (31) await nightfall when they feed. Southern Africa has no less than 75 species of bat of which eight are fruit-eating. They play an important role in the ecology of any region although the details and implications of this are not yet fully understood and southern Africa's rich bat fauna is still something of an enigma.

30   31

There are an estimated 3 000 to 4 000 giraffe in the Kruger National Park (32, 33), several hundred in the nearby Timbavati Nature Reserve famous for its 'white' lions, and some have been successfully reintroduced into Natal's wildlife reserves. But the giraffe's fortunes have not always been so good and at the turn of the century, farmers took a heavy toll. They used the animal's bones for fertiliser and its hide for whips. Today, however, the giraffe is protected and browses, unmolested by man, among the tree tops.

Normally the males are about five metres tall and the females about four. The giraffe's long neck evolved as the animal literally reached for a niche in the trees, away from competition from other leaf eaters. The neck has no more bones in it than man or most other vertebrates, however, in the case of the giraffe these seven vertebrae are greatly extended and jointed in such a way that the neck is amazingly flexible. The distance of the creature's head from the rest of its body and the demands of a body which can weigh up to a ton, place special stresses on the heart. Therefore it comes as no surprise that the giraffe has the largest heart in the animal world – an adult's can have a mass of 12 kilograms.

The heart works hard to drive blood to the animal's head and the jugular vein which is two centimetres in diameter and lined with special valves prevents the blood from rushing back to the heart and lungs. On the other hand, when the giraffe stoops to drink, the system must prevent a return rush of blood to the head. Powerful valves at the base of the brain and the complex arrangement of blood vessels cushion the shock of any drastic pressure changes.

Although the giraffe is a harmless animal, the bulls fight, presumably for dominance and a claim to the fertile females. They pound one another with their heavy knobbed skulls which they use almost as sledgehammers on their long swinging necks. The fight ends when one of the combatants accepts defeat and lopes off. Because the female's skull is not armed with knobs, she defends herself and her young with her formidable hooves. Lion, which sometimes prey on giraffe, are understandably wary of their kick.

The giraffe well illustrates the immense diversity of wild-life – ungulates in particular – that evolved on the African savannahs as a result of the great number of plant species. But it is not only the number of different animal species that is amazing; the overall mass of animals supported by the grasslands of Africa is unequalled.

The grasses offer so many opportunities – and the wild-life has come to use them so effectively – that even creatures which seem to be sharing the same grazing grounds are invariably proven on closer inspection to be consuming different plants. In the case of wildebeest and zebra, for instance, they are eating different parts of plants and therefore are not competing in the true sense for the primary product. Of course there is overlap and, as the season becomes drier each year before the rains, there is less food from which to choose and the competiton becomes fiercer. The giraffe though, with its larder safely among the thorns above the heads of the other animals can dine relatively undisturbed.

THE HIGHVELD

Probably no area in South Africa has lost as much of its wildlife heritage as has the Highveld. Here, as on the immense expanses of the Karoo, there were once great herds of game feeding on the rich and verdant grasslands. A painting by the famous hunter and naturalist, Sir William Cornwallis Harris, reveals the slopes of the Magaliesberg literally dotted with elephant.

While urban sprawl has wiped out most of the big game, the suburban gardens of Johannesburg and the Witwatersrand have created new habitats for a far richer birdlife than formerly existed. More than 150 species are on record in the area.

The Braamfontein Spruit, of which one tributary rises at the foot of the densest highrise area in the southern hemisphere, Hillbrow, shelters a surprising array of wildlife as it meanders through the suburbs. Thus even for the urban dweller there is scope to explore. Traces of the nocturnal genet, a long-bodied carnivore little larger than a domestic cat and which feeds on rats, mice and birds, can often be found. Shortly after a recent summer downpour, a water leguaan was spotted crossing a main road. In many Johannesburg suburbs, the spotted eagle owl has taken up residence, its low gruff hoot breaking the darkness of evening.

At the Melville Koppies Nature Reserve – a magnificent area of near-virgin Highveld close to Johannesburg's city centre – there are mongoose, guineafowl and a great number of small forms of wildlife, not to mention the wonders of the insect world, to reward the patient observer.

The open Highveld grasslands were once the home to herds of blesbok (34), today still common in some of the local wildlife reserves. Several farmers have restocked parts of their holdings with this antelope which provides meat for commercial purposes. The concept of hunting animals in what are essentially sanctuaries is abhorrent to many; however, with land at a premium, often the only justification for maintaining herds of wild game is economic.

In many ways the white-tailed gnu or black wildebeest (35) is an incongruous creature; its massive forequarters and great shaggy head contrasting sharply with slender hindquarters. Distinguished by its white tail, this gnu has been reintroduced to many reserves and is gradually increasing in number after a long period of decline when it was often hunted.

Surprisingly, the Magaliesberg still harbours much of the wildlife found there 150 years ago. Animals such as Burchell's zebra (36) had to be reintroduced, but in this rugged range just 40 kilometres from Johannesburg there are still leopard, brown hyaena, kudu, otter, jackal, warthog and baboon. Negotiations are under way to make the Magaliesberg a single, large nature reserve open to the public – a wonderful asset to the densely-populated regions of the Witwatersrand.

34

35

In the wild, cheetah (37) are seldom seen for they have large territories and therefore tend to be widely dispersed. Although fairly successful on the hunt – provided they can bring down their prey within a 500 metre sprint for they do not have great stamina – they often lose their kills to more aggressive animals such as wild dog, lion and hyaena.

These strikingly marked and elegant creatures are still to be found at the Suikerbosrand Nature Reserve and at the special cheetah park in the foothills of the Magaliesberg.

The muscular caracal or African lynx (38) is geared for speed and agility.

Cunning, elegant and solitary, the leopard (39) stalks the wild areas even just outside several of South Africa's major cities. Their secretive ways account for their rarely being seen and they tend to spend the daylight hours either up a tree, or snoozing in mountain clefts or in lairs under dense bush. On the hunt, the leopard either ambushes his victim from an overhanging tree or stalks his prey on the ground. The carcass is often hauled up into the branches, safely away from the unwelcome attentions of hungry lions or hyaena. Of all the African big cats, leopard are the most likely to attack man – and there are many reports of such attacks made with deadly stealth, usually from the rear.

38

39

South Africa has two species of leguaan or monitor lizard (40): the water leguaan and the tree leguaan. The tree leguaan seen here is about a metre in length. When cornered it uses its tail like a whip and puts on an admirable display of aggression. The tree leguaan is a carnivore with a penchant for birds' eggs, chicks and insects. Like snakes, leguaans have forked tongues with which they smell.

The vervet monkeys' ingenuity is being tested to the utmost in the battle for survival since their taste for fruit brings them directly into conflict with farmers. They exist a few kilometres outside Johannesburg but are not frequently seen.

Although the vervet (41) is an arboreal creature, it does not need dense forest; indeed it can live quite successfully in fairly open country as long as it has a tree close at hand as a ready escape route.

The African hedgehog (42) is one of those widespread creatures found throughout South Africa and yet because of its nocturnal ways is seldom seen.

41

40 42

Regal of bearing and a splendid jumper, the kudu (43) is plentiful in South Africa. Even in the Cape, roadside signs warn motorists of the hazard of leaping kudu at night when they are difficult to see. Retiring by nature, the kudu lives in wooded areas where it browses, often on plants poisonous to other species.

The springbok (44) is essentially an antelope of the dry regions such as the Kalahari and Karoo, but it has been widely introduced onto Highveld wildlife reserves and farms for it shows great promise as a source of revenue. Compared to domestic cattle, the springbok is many more times as efficient at converting grasses to protein and seldom tries to escape from captivity.

The eland (45, 46) must have been at home on the Highveld in times past, although it too does well in the drier parts of the country. This massive antelope can weigh more than a ton and many attempts – some partly successful – have been made to domesticate it. Besides providing immense quantities of meat, its milk is highly nutritious and rich in cream.

In terms of the number of people bitten, the puff-adder is South Africa's most dangerous snake (47). Yet it is not aggressive. The reason for the high bite rate is that puff-adders like sunning themselves on footpaths and open areas where they are likely to come into contact with humans. They will only attack if actually trodden on or molested in some way.

They are common in South Africa and despite their somewhat sluggish ways are believed to be among the fastest-striking snakes in Africa. Their fangs can be up to two centimetres in length and the poison they inject into their victims is haematoxic and causes intense pain and swelling, often leading to death unless the person receives prompt attention.

The puff-adder's normal diet is frogs and rodents, thus it plays an important role in controlling rodent populations. They are born fully formed – sometimes as many as 30 at a time – and are dangerous from the moment of birth.

All snakes must slough their skins in order to grow, as this common tiger snake is seen doing (48). Once the snake becomes larger, it simply wriggles out of its outgrown skin and slithers away in a new set of scales.

This nocturnal snake is easily aroused but it is very much a case of its hiss being worse than its bite. It will strike and hiss persistently, and puts up a most aggressive display, but its venom is weak and of limited danger to humans. Its diet consists mainly of rodents and lizards.

Unfortunately man generally regards snakes with fear and hostility and reacts by killing them. Yet only 12 out of the 157 species found in South Africa possess poison lethal to man. And, all snakes, given the option, would rather flee than fight. Generally only those that are in some way molested are provoked into attack.

47 48

Gliding smoothly down to a kill, a Cape vulture (49) shows its skills in the air. This magnificent bird is a common sight in many of the rural Highveld areas.

During the last few decades, the Cape vulture has found its existence increasingly jeopardised. With the decline of the game herds – and with them the predators – the Cape vulture found its source of food steadily diminishing.

Observers noticed, however, that Cape vulture populations were declining essentially because the chicks were rickety and tended to break their wings once they tried to leave the nest. This led researchers to discover that the tiny splinters of bone left behind by scavenging hyaenas at a kill are vital to the chicks' proper development and that the adult birds carry the calcium-rich chips back to the chicks in the nest.

As a result of the changes to its habitat, the Cape vulture was in danger of dying out in a range which it had patrolled as self-appointed refuse remover for centuries. In an attempt to solve the problem, vulture 'restaurants' were created. At specially fenced off sites, carcasses and smashed-up bone fragments are left for the birds. The Cape vulture chicks are now receiving a better calcium supply and the plunge to extinction has been slowed.

The sacred ibis (50) is a common sight, even in Johannesburg's suburbs. A frequent inhabitant of Highveld gardens is the lovely bokmakierie (51) with its familiar calls. Now fairly common in Johannesburg's northern suburbs, the grey loerie (52) is normally a Bushveld bird found north of the Magaliesberg.

51

52

THE ARID WEST

Westwards the Highveld gradually gives way to the great Kalahari, a vast basin characterised by deep sand and limestone outcrops, and by hundreds of shallow salt pans, each bed covered in blinding white sediment. In the heat of midday, watery mirages dance mockingly over the plains while each passing game herd or dust devil sends the talcum-fine dust billowing into the air. Yet in the stillness of pre-dawn, temperatures can plummet to freeze the traveller's water bottles solid and leave in the air a coldness that clouds the breath until well after sunrise. From horizon to horizon the grass waves interrupted by the occasional acacia tree, by fossil sand dunes and, rarely, by water.

Still further west the Kalahari blends with the northern extensions of another arid region, the Great Karoo. Between here and the Atlantic seaboard lies Namaqualand, famous for the magical metamorphosis its desiccated landscape undergoes in years when some rain falls and sets it ablaze with carpets of wildflowers.

The fauna of the west is wonderfully adapted to the region's harsh climate. Though the game herds of the area are today found mainly in such places as the magnificent Kalahari Gemsbok National Park the smaller animals can be seen everywhere.

Often one of the first animals that the visitor to the Kalahari encounters is the grey meerkat, or suricate (53). These highly social members of the mongoose family take up residence in the disused warrens of ground squirrels or old termite mounds; here they can be seen as they sit erect on their haunches sunning themselves or suspiciously eyeing any intruder. Birds of prey are a dreaded enemy and the colony keeps a special alert; as soon as one is spotted the meerkats scramble helter-skelter back into the safety of their burrow.

Most famous of all South African antelope is the springbok (54). That these graceful gazelle have given their name to so many things South African is not surprising. In the grasslands of South Africa's drier areas herds of a hundred or more can be seen grazing as they move slowly across the veld. Should the breeze bring the smell of a predator or the herd be frightened for some reason, the onlooker will be treated to a display of spectacular behaviour unique to the springbok: the animals begin to pronk (from the Afrikaans word: to show off) – they leap stiff-legged through the air to heights of up to three metres and at the same time spread a fan of pure white fur on the hindquarters. It is a sight never to be forgotten as the veld erupts into a mass of bobbing white patches and airborne springbok.

Once springbok occurred in far greater numbers, and over an even greater area of South Africa. The trekkers told of herds of hundreds of thousands that would at times migrate great distances in search of grazing. Though hunting and land development decimated those great herds of yesterday, the springbok is today increasing again in numbers, particularly as it does better than cattle in very dry areas and farmers have begun to keep them.

The springbok can make do with surprisingly little water when necessary, going for weeks at a time without it by obtaining its moisture requirements from the vegetation it eats, which apart from grass also consists of roots and bulbs dug up with its hooves.

Perhaps strangest of all the sights the arid west offers is the huge communal nest of social weavers (55) looming massive among the branches of camelthorn acacias. These enormous grass structures – often several cubic metres in volume – comprise dozens of separate nesting chambers, each with its own entrance and housing a pair of birds. Amazingly these giant nests begin with a single pair of birds laying stalks of dry grass along a branch. As the seasons and years pass, the nest is constantly added to by other social weavers. Often finches and other small birds will take up residence in unused chambers, whilst owls and eagles find the flat top of the structure a splendid site for their own nests. Mice find the grass mass a cosy habitat, and snakes and rats arrive to raid the nest chambers for chicks. All in all the social weavers' nest presents a remarkable community of animals, and is well worth close observation.

One social weaver's nest is known to have been in use for more than a century, but more usually the host tree dies or simply collapses under the strain.

The ground squirrel (56) is another gregarious animal, living in communities of up to 30 or more. These attractive rodents which excavate elaborate underground burrow systems in even the hardest and rockiest soils, constantly forage a wide area in the vicinity of the nest in search of suitable plants and roots. They delicately hold their food between their forepaws as they nibble away. Whilst foraging they erect their bushy tails above their bodies in parasol fashion, partly as a shade against the severe Kalahari sun and partly to camouflage themselves from the many sharp-eyed birds of prey that abound in the Kalahari skies.

55   56

According to African legend the red hartebeest (57, 58) was the last animal to be given horns. Unfortunately the Creator was by then hard put to think up yet another new design, and also in a great hurry to finish the job. The result was that all he did was take two misshapen old bones and place them willy-nilly on the hartebeest's head. But if he lost out on his horns, this widely dispersed inhabitant of the Kalahari made up for it in the beauty of its coat, in speed and in stamina. Despite his awkward-looking gait the red hartebeest is reputed to be one of the fleetest of all antelopes. While hunting drastically reduced its numbers, today the red hartebeest is common again in the arid west, and several fine herds grace the sandy plains of the Kalahari Gemsbok National Park.

For the Kalahari lion (59) conditions are very different from those in the Kruger National Park where the hunt is short and prey plentiful. In the Kalahari, however, life is not so easy. Prey is nowhere near as abundant, and there is little cover from which the victim can be stalked. Few trees for shade and the scarcity of water make survival still more difficult. It is hardly surprising that researchers have found that more than 50 per cent of the Kalahari lion's diet consists of small mammals including porcupines. There are cases on record of desperately hungry Kalahari lions tackling porcupines and suffering an agonising and slow death from infected mouth and tongue wounds.

If threatened the 'pocket dragon', the sungazer lizard (60), rolls itself into a ball, gripping its tail between its jaws, presenting a formidable coat of spiny armour.

To attract prey, the horned adder (61) buries itself in soft sand, leaving only its head and the tip of the tail exposed. The vibrating tail attracts the lizards that form its prey.

The Namaqualand chameleon (62) hides by drawing in the sides of his body, flattening it laterally, and aligning himself with the sun so as to cast the least possible shadow. He also alters the patterns and markings of his body to match almost perfectly those of the veld. Yet should he be discovered, he fights back spectacularly: hissing, snapping, inflating himself, and even leaping in a desperate effort to bluff his foe into retreating.

61

62

Herds of blue wildebeest (*previous page*) are yet another magnificent feature of the Kalahari, seasonally migrating great distances in order to exploit the best grazing. The wildebeest is an odd-looking animal to say the least. Cornwallis Harris once described it as having the forequarters of an ox, the hindquarters of an antelope, and the tail of a horse. African folklore tells that the Great Creator made up the wildebeest from all the spare parts He had left over.

One of the arid west's most endearing animals is the bat-eared fox (64), whose huge ears and cheeky blackened face make it an instant favourite. Insects make up the greater part of its diet – a scorpion or millipede moving in its underground burrow is easily and accurately pin-pointed with those huge ears and promptly dug up.

Scavengers at a kill may seem gruesome to us but one must not forget their crucial role in the recycling of organic matter. Nature has evolved a highly complex relationship between the various scavengers. These white-backed vultures (65) are amongst the last to feed on a carcass. They spot the kill from their high altitude holding stations and glide down to pick the remaining scraps of flesh from the carcass and ingest fragments of bone left by the spotted hyaenas.

The brown hyaena (66) is a common scavenger, though rarely seen. These wary animals usually hunt alone after dark – they feed on anything from the oldest carrion to insects and sea-shore detritus. The Afrikaans name, *Strandwolf* (beach wolf), derives from the observations of the early settlers at the Cape.

64

65

The remarkable ostrich (67), the largest of all birds can weigh well over 150 kg and run at a sustained speed of at least 40 km/h (with peak speeds in excess of 70 km/h). They defend themselves and their chicks with powerful forward kicks of their dagger-clawed feet. The loud booming voice of the male can sound terrifyingly like the roar of a lion.

The nest is a mere scrape in the sand constructed by both the male and the female who take turns in incubating the 15-20 enormous eggs. The predominantly black-plumed male takes the night-watch and the inconspicuously coloured female sits during the day. Once the chicks have hatched they move off with their parents often joining up with other parent groups to form 'nursery' groups of up to 80 or more chicks and a few adult birds.

The photograph shows a small nursery group led by a displaying male and followed by two females.

The bateleur (68) is a most striking eagle and its name (from the French for acrobat) is particularly appropriate in view of this bird's habit of performing spectacular acrobatics, including somersaults, dives and slow rolls. Fond of the carrion of small animals it can sometimes be seen along the roadside feeding upon the remains of small mammals killed by motor vehicles.

68

The gemsbok (*following page*) is undoubtedly the arid west's most magnificent antelope. These sleek and hardy antelope can live almost indefinitely on no more water than that which they derive from the grasses and melons that form their food.

The gemsbok has evolved some remarkable physiological adaptations in order to cope with the intense heat and aridity of the desert. Since shade is scarce, each day it must tolerate temperatures of more than 40°C, letting the heat build up during the day and then losing it at night. A remarkable heat exchange system built into the moist nasal passages cools down blood on its way to the brain in order to avoid damage to this heat-sensitive organ. With liquid at a premium, moisture lost through panting and sweating is kept to an absolute minimum.

The gemsbok is often said to have been the origin of the fabled unicorn, and as the photograph shows, a side on view of those rapier horns does indeed make them appear as one.

NATAL AND THE DRAKENSBERG

The Zulu called the great Drakensberg 'quath-lamba', the barrier of spears. This range of mountains runs southwards for more than 500 km, abruptly dividing the Highveld's grassy plains to its west from the warm and wooded land of Natal to its east. Beyond the Drakensberg the land slowly falls away to form a verdant coastal plain bordering the warm Indian Ocean. In northern Natal there are still great areas of undeveloped land, and several fine wildlife reserves, harbouring a great variety of wildlife in magnificent habitat.

Hippo (70, 71) abound in the many wide rivers that wind their way across the densely-forested Natal coastal plain, as well as in the network of adjoining pans that the flooding rivers fill each rainy season. They are also plentiful in the shining coastal lakes that are such a feature of northern Natal. Hippo are remarkable animals on many accounts, not least of which is their size. Weighing up to two and a half tons or more, these massive ungulates are truly amphibious, seldom moving more than a few kilometres away from water. As their specific gravity is slightly greater than that of water, hippo are able to control their buoyancy at will by simply regulating the volume of air in their great bodies; a little more retained air in the lungs and the hippo floats, swimming if necessary. A little less retained air and this 'river-horse' (as aptly described by its name, derived from the Greek) sinks, to be able to tip-toe along the bottom with all the grace of a ballet dancer. Hippo can actually stay submerged for up to six minutes, moving a considerable distance under water.

They can even give birth to their young under water (a hippo calf weighing 60-80 kilograms!) and suckle them there too if necessary.

In the water, a hippo's broad back presents a convenient perch and feeding site for various birds. Egrets and ox-peckers feast on the numerous skin parasites, while wagtails are attracted by aquatic insects. Terrapins (water tortoises) like to bask on it, often several at a time. Though hippo generally spend daytime in the water they will, when the water is cold, emerge to warm themselves in the sun, at times even suffering sunburn. Hippo do eat a certain amount of aquatic vegetation, but at dusk leave their watery retreat and make their way by well-worn pathways to graze in the surrounding areas, consuming in the region of 100 kg of greenery in a single night.

It is at night, too, that hippo bulls sometimes engage in terrible fights, lashing out at one another with their enormously long canine teeth and bellowing loudly. Whether roused or not, hippo should never be approached closely either on water or on land for they are likely to defend themselves viciously. Not a few people have lost their lives to those wicked canines, particularly at night, when the light of a lamp seems to confuse the creatures. To come between a retreating hippo and the water is asking for trouble.

Neighbour to the hippo is the Nile crocodile (*previous page*), a reptilian monster that has come to us almost unchanged since the time of the dinosaurs. Growing to almost six metres, these armour-plated giants among today's reptiles have a vital part to play if the ecology of river and lake systems is to remain healthy. Crocodiles feed mainly on fish, primarily barbel and bream and usually only the larger specimens. Because these fish prey on smaller species and on juveniles, it is necessary that their numbers be kept in check and here the crocodile is an important agent. Although this is a simplified view of this extremely complex ecological picture, it is clear that any reduction in the number of crocodiles will have far-reaching consequences on the fish population.

Although their appearance might not suggest it, crocodiles are very conscientious mothers and spend long periods guarding their riverbank nests (73) against predators such as monitor lizards. When her 60-80 eggs begin to hatch (75), a mother crocodile responds to the squeaking call of her young, unearthing the buried clutch by means of her hind legs and gently encouraging the newborn into her mouth. She then carries them down to the water for their first swim. Of the many young she produces, very few reach maturity for they are preyed upon by a host of animals.

Seemingly placid at the water's edge this crocodile (74) could explode into action should a suitable animal come within reach. The crocodile uses its heavy muscular tail as a counterweight to fling itself out of the water and grab the snout of its victim, dragging it beneath the water and drowning it. The idea that a crocodile keeps an underwater 'larder' is without foundation, for the reptile will not eat food that is putrid.

Greater flamingos massed on Lake St Lucia (76) are one of the more spectacular sights to be seen on this large coastal lake. These birds feed in water that is sufficiently shallow for them to submerge the entire head. In the process the bird's remarkable bill comes into its own. The tongue, working like a lightning-quick piston, tirelessly thrusts water containing the minute aquatic organisms on which the bird lives through the special screening structures within the bill, so trapping the foodstuff. And as the flamingo moves slowly through the shallows its feet stir up the bottom organisms for the tongue and bill to sieve.

Flamingos do not breed on Natal's lakes; they wing thousands of kilometres across the subcontinent and as far north as the bitter soda lakes of the Great Rift Valley to

build their nests of mud. In the long term the safety such inhospitable areas offer from predators offsets the years when conditions are so hostile that the birds fail to breed at all or subsequently lose thousands of chicks when the waters dry up too quickly.

For many game watchers the cry of the fish eagle (77) is as symbolic of Africa's wild places as the trumpeting of an elephant. Like all eagles it has amazingly keen vision and can swoop to take a fish from the water surface, or just beneath it, accurately compensating for the effects of light diffraction. Having made its catch, the fish eagle flies (78) to its favourite perch to consume its meal. A large fish eagle has been seen to carry off an almost metre-long crocodile.

Many people overlook frogs as a form of wildlife, but today a growing number of wildlife lovers are discovering the enjoyment of observing South Africa's wealth of smaller creatures. The colouring of some frogs is as beautiful as that of butterflies, and this is particularly the case with the reed frogs, found in warm, low-lying areas, mostly in the eastern regions of South Africa. The painted reed frog (79) comes in a great variety of colours and patterns, depending upon the area in which it lives. Using their long legs and suckered feet these three-centimetre-long rainbows leap about vegetation, capturing small flying insects such as

mosquitoes. Like most frogs they catch their prey by flicking out a sticky tongue. Only male frogs have a voice and in the case of the painted reed frog it is a short piercing whistle repeated endlessly from after sunset until the early hours of the morning.

A male raucous toad (80) calls from a vlei, attracting females to the area. With each call, the air moves from the creature's lungs over the vocal chords and into the resonant vocal sac seen here fully inflated. The air is then returned to the lungs and the process repeated. To a beetle or other

potential prey, a raucous toad on the hunt (83) must be a formidable looking monster.

The common river frog (81) is found over most of South Africa except for the arid regions, its nightly croaking radiating from many a suburban garden pond.

The Cape river frog (82) is another widely distributed South African amphibian. River frogs are closely related to the European edible frog that for so long has delighted the palates of the French.

Impala (84, 85) are not restricted only to the Transvaal Lowveld – they also occur plentifully in Natal. These antelope are well known for the spectacularly long and graceful leaps they make.

Another attraction for which the Natal wildlife reserves are noted is the nyala (86), a close relative of the kudu and with a similar regal bearing, being strikingly marked with a rather shaggy coat. Like the kudu it feeds mostly by browsing. Nyala are seldom seen far from water, and they make their home in warm, low-lying wooded areas. They are also common along the Levubu River of the Kruger National Park in the northern Transvaal.

84

85   86

88
87　89

Fifty years ago the white rhino (87, 89) came within a hair's breadth of extinction in the wild. This short-sighted, rather docile, and second largest of all land animals fell in great numbers to hunters greedy to make a fortune from rhino horn. In the East it is believed, entirely without foundation, that rhino horn acts as an aphrodisiac.

Had it not been for the tsetse fly killing off the hunters' horses in areas of Natal, and thereby safeguarding this creature in these areas, the white rhino would almost certainly be extinct today. Fortunately Natal conservationists came to the rescue and as a result of a highly successful campaign there are today white rhino to spare for transloca-tion to wildlife reserves in areas where they have not been seen for a century or more.

In colour the white rhino differs little from the black rhino (88), its somewhat smaller (and very much shorter-tempered) relative. It has been suggested that the word 'white' is actually derived from the word 'wide', for indeed the white rhino does have a particularly broad muzzle, being strictly a grazer and needing large lips to tear out grass. The black rhino on the other hand has a distinctly pointed mouth, using its prehensile upper lip to pluck leaves and twigs.

Among the lonely peaks and gorges of the Drakensberg there survives a great deal of wildlife. Dassies, or hyraxes (90), are a common sight as they scurry up near-vertical rock faces using their friction-padded feet kept moist by special glands. Amazingly these little vegetarians are close relatives of the elephant and share several features although obviously on a much smaller scale.

Dassies form the main prey of the black eagle (91), a magnificent bird with a two-metre wingspan found in mountainous areas.

The bald ibis (92) today finds its only refuge in the Drakensberg where it nests on the ledges of rock faces. There are probably less than 2 000 left.

90 91 92

94
95
93 96

Though South Africa has several hundred species of spider only two are in any way dangerous to man – the button or black widow spider and the recluse spider – and even these very rarely so. Spiders play a vital role in helping to keep insect populations in check. The female giant orb-web spider (93) spins her large round web of golden silk between shrubs or trees, trapping all manner of flying insects. As is the case with most spiders, the male is a fraction of his wife's size, and can often be found moving cautiously about her web.

The net-throwing spider (94) is a strange denizen of Natal's coastal dune forests. Suspending itself a few centimetres above the ground, it spins a mesh of sticky silk between its two front pairs of legs and waits for a crawling insect to pass below. When that happens, the spider instantly drops to the ground, at the same time casting its net over the victim in a manner reminiscent of the ancient Roman gladiators.

Also a member of the orb-web group of spiders, this species (95) constructs her somewhat smaller web in marshy areas.

Even among spiders there are keen fishermen. The nursery-web spider (96), seen here guarding her newly hatched offspring, lives on the surface of ponds and streams, diving to catch small fish and tadpoles.

T HE CAPE

It is difficult to imagine now, but three centuries ago when the Dutch first settled at the Cape they found elephants wandering where Adderley Street is today. Hippo and crocodiles lazed in the rivers, lions padded the beaches, and the cry of the fish eagle resounded across the slopes of Table Mountain. Almost daily, early naturalists at the Cape discovered animals new to them – this was one of science's first opportunities to get to know the wildlife of Africa well. The extent of their work is reflected in the number of animals that today bear the prefix 'Cape' to their common names, even though the species is often found far and wide across the continent.

Today there is still a great variety of wildlife to be found throughout the Cape Province, with a number of species unique to the area. The Cape Department of Nature Conservation administers numerous protected wildlife areas, such as the outstanding Cape Point Nature Reserve. Here, as well as in many other mountainous areas of the Cape, chacma baboons (97) are commonly seen, often along main roads. Sadly, thoughtless motorists have encouraged some of these primates to solicit food which has led to unnaturally aggressive behaviour and ill health from the change in diet.

Living in troops of up to 200 individuals, with a well-defined social structure, chacma baboons feed mainly on grass, roots, fruit and other vegetable matter. They eat insects too, including scorpions. The remarkable adaptability of these animals is illustrated by the fact that in the Cape Point Nature Reserve they have learned to forage along the sea shore at low tide, feeding on shellfish and other seafood. The photograph shows a pair of chacma baboons preening, an act that has important social implications.

Beyond the mountains that separate the Cape's seaboard from its interior lie the arid plains of the Karoo, broken periodically by yet more mountains. The mountain zebra (98) is smaller and more agile than his Lowveld relative, the Burchell's zebra, and is very much at home in dry areas. In the Mountain Zebra National Park near Cradock these handsome little zebra have recovered from near extinction only 40 years ago, and in the Park's protection have multiplied into several fine herds. They have hooves that grow rapidly to offset the abrasive effects of their rocky habitat, and they can be identified by the lack of stripes under the belly.

97 98

Widespread throughout southern Africa, the little steenbok (99) can often be seen in the Cape, grazing and browsing at all times of day, and always alone except when paired in the breeding season. They can run fast when alarmed and sometimes take shelter in a disused aardvark burrow.

The handsome bontebok (100) is a species unique to the Cape. Having been saved from certain extinction by conservation-minded farmers in the 1930s, it is now breeding well (101) in the Bontebok National Park near Swellendam, from which animals can be translocated to stock other reserves. The bontebok resembles, and is closely related to, the more common blesbok of the Highveld. The two are considered by zoologists to be members of the same species, which has through geographic separation evolved different markings.

99 101

100

Like others of their species, the inhabitants of the Addo Elephant National Park happily abandon themselves to the joys of a mud wallow (102) whenever the occasion allows. Located near Port Elizabeth, this park protects Africa's most southerly breeding elephant population, considered by some to be a sub-species of the African elephant.

Addo is a national park with an interesting history, for here, among the impenetrable bush and spekboom thickets, a mass slaughter once took place that almost wiped out the elephants in the region. Due to numerous complaints from farmers that the elephants were trampling their crops and terrorising people, the Administrator of the Cape in 1920, Sir Frederic de Waal, instructed the famous hunter Major Pretorius to shoot all the elephants. After eleven months in what he called 'a hunter's hell' Major Pretorius had shot 120 of the animals, fighting his way through the dense and claw-ing bush. But fortunately the people of Port Elizabeth decided that they had had enough of the slaughter and had it stopped. The remaining 23 elephants, by now extremely wary of man, and with a reputation for being ill-tempered, remained hidden in the thick bush. By the time the Addo Elephant National Park was proclaimed in 1931 their numbers had dwindled to 11. Fortunately the pachyderms responded well to being conserved and today the number of elephant in the Addo Park has increased to more than 200, making translocation of some to other areas necessary.

The Addo elephants (103) show some interesting peculiarities. They breed more than four times as frequently as elephants in the Kruger National Park, and only the bulls possess tusks, and these are very small. Also, probably due to their having to move about relatively little in search of food, they have a thicker layer of fat.

102 103

The Cape buffalo (105) grazes mainly between sunset and sunrise, preferring to spend the day hidden among dense vegetation. Though these massive bovines have relatively poor sight and hearing, they have a very keen sense of smell, particularly when it comes to lion, their main predator. The Addo Elephant National Park is home to the only Cape buffalo herds still found in the Cape.

Another creature of the night is the spotted eagle owl (104), which can often be seen between dusk and dawn on telephone poles or other vantage points from which it hunts rodents and insects. Found from the Cape to northern Africa these useful birds are happy to take up residence in household gardens providing they are not molested.

Bushpigs (106) are nocturnal inhabitants of forests such as Tsitsikama and other densely wooded areas, being slightly smaller than the warthog, South Africa's only other wild member of the pig family.

The Cape clawless otter (107) inhabits rivers, streams and sheltered coastal waters. Powerful swimmers, these carnivores grow to a metre in length and feed mainly on crabs and fish, for which they are able to dive and remain in pursuit under water for up to two and a half minutes. Like South Africa's other otter, the spotted-necked otter of the Lowveld and Natal, this species has partially webbed feet and is able to use its front feet to grasp its prey while feeding.

The Cape pangolin (108), yet another nocturnal animal, has powerful digging claws to excavate the nests of termites and ants, on whose inhabitants it feeds with its long and sticky tongue. When alarmed, these strange mammals roll themselves into a ball, presenting a continuous armour of overlapping scales, which are actually highly modified hairs.

The Cape has more kinds of tortoise than anywhere else in the world; in one district alone five species exist side by side. The photograph (109) shows an 8-cm-long member of the geometric tortoise group, enjoying a daisy. Since they were almost eliminated by pet trade collectors who used to export thousands to England and Europe, some rare members of this group are now carefully protected in special reserves on private Western Cape farms.

The Cape dormouse (110) is just one of the hundreds of small mammals that, though common and every bit as fascinating as the larger animals, are a largely overlooked form of wildlife. Nocturnal in habits, the Cape dormouse feeds on berries, seeds and insects, and seldom enters houses, although it sometimes shows up around campfires to collect food scraps.

106

107 108 110

109

112
113
111 114

Of the almost 900 species of birds recorded from South Africa, a good many of these are to be seen in the Cape. Some of the more common species are the long-tailed widow bird (111), lanner falcon (112), pied kingfisher (113), cattle egret (114), blue crane (115) and malachite sunbird (116). The blue crane is South Africa's national bird and appears on the five cent coin.

115

116

Black-footed wildcats (117) are slightly smaller than their domestic counterparts and notoriously 'wild' in temperament. They are inhabitants of dry areas such as the Karoo, where their habit of living in hollow termite mounds has earned them the local name of 'anthill tigers'. They are nocturnal and feed mainly on rodents. This pair was photographed in the recently established Karoo National Park near Beaufort West. South Africa's other wildcat is the African wildcat, which in many areas has extensively interbred with stray domestic cats and is therefore seldom found in its pure form.

The nocturnal porcupine (118) is Africa's largest rodent, using its gnawing teeth to feed on roots, bulbs, berries, tree bark and other vegetable matter. When alarmed, a porcupine produces a loud rattling sound by wagging its stubby tail covered in special hollow quills. At the same time it erects the formidable array of rigid, needle-sharp quills on its back and sides. Should this threat go unheeded, the porcupine will make a backwards charge at its aggressor, embedding the quills, which detach readily from their sockets to bring excruciating pain and sometimes fatal infection. Porcupines usually give birth to single young, the quills being soft and flexible at birth.

117 118

OUR SEASHORES

South Africa's 3 000 kilometre shoreline is probably one of the most diverse any country could offer. Washed by the warm southward-flowing Moçambique current of the Indian Ocean, the east coast boasts endless tropical beaches where giant turtles come to nest, and coral reefs as good as those off Kenya. On the opposite side of the continent, South Africa's west coast is very different. The Atlantic Ocean's icy Benguella current arrives nutrient-rich from the Antarctic to bring a chill to the land and incredible fertility to the sea. The grey skies seem to stretch forever and the constant wind has a bite of loneliness and desolation. Little rain falls and it is here that the Namib Desert begins.

Between these two extremes there lie all manner of shores – some rocky, others sandy – and all the way along there are mounds of kitchen refuse left by prehistoric people. These middens of sea shells, animal and fish bones, some pottery, stone tools and even what appear to be stone fishing sinkers, reflect the life of the people in those ancient times and the wealth of coastal wildlife that surrounded them.

The sea is a natural resource which no country can afford to squander and South Africa, like so many others, has been slow to realise the importance of conserving its coastal habitats. A great step forward was taken with the proclamation of the Tsitsikama National Coastal Park along the southern Cape. This 70-kilometre stretch of unspoiled seashore lies midway between the cold west and the warm

east, resulting in a particularly great variety of seashore animals, and creating one of our finest parks.

In 1977, St Croix Island off Port Elizabeth was declared a marine reserve to protect its 25 000-strong colony of jackass penguins (119). This bird is unique to South Africa, breeding mainly on Dassen Island, off the Atlantic coast. Though seemingly clumsy on land, the jackass penguin is very much at home in the sea, using its flipper-like wings to 'fly' through the water and steering with its webbed feet. Penguins feed on fish, their normal diet consisting of pilchards and anchovies of which they eat great quantities. For some years the number of penguins along the South African coast has been declining and although overfishing by commercial trawlers is often blamed, it seems that the past practice of collecting huge numbers of their eggs for sale has harmed them more. This was stopped in 1968.

Inshore coastal waters, particularly estuaries, are the breeding grounds for a great many fish species. It is true to say that with our estuaries ruined by pollution and industrial development, the great oceanic fish shoals would soon disappear, for no young fish (120) would ever reach the sea.

Along the rocky coasts divers can snorkel in countless tide pools, allowing close-up views of such unusual animals as feather duster worms (121), with their plumes that trap plankton; and sea stars (122) that feed on molluscs.

120

121

122

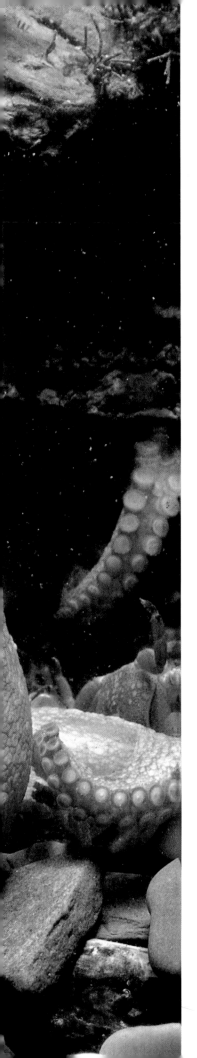

The common octopus (123) is another denizen of our coastal tide pools, feeding mainly on crabs and swimming to safety at the least sign of danger. It propels itself by means of a water jet on each side of its body, and though it can grow up to one metre in total width, it is harmless to man. Strangely, the octopus is a mollusc and therefore closely related to slugs and snails, yet research has shown it to have the eyesight and intelligence of much higher animals.

The brown rock crab (124) is the commonest of all crabs along our rocky shores, and is a favourite food of the octopus and shore birds. At night these little crustaceans venture high up the shore and a torchlight inspection will often reveal them feeding, or moulting their shells as they grow.

Further from the shore, remaining submerged even at low tide, lives the basket star (125), often found, as the picture shows, clinging to the fronds of a bright red sea-fan coral. The basket star is a member of the starfish family, while the sea-fan is related to the sea anemone.

124

125

On a warm and moonlit summer's night there is a strange and wonderful ritual to be witnessed along the remote sandy beaches of northern Natal. It is the nesting of turtles; the 1,4-metre-long loggerhead and the 2-metre-long leatherback. Encrusted with barnacles, these massive reptiles haul themselves from the sea and bulldoze their way up the beach, heaving and sighing as they use their ill-suited flippers to reach the area above the high water mark.

Each female then begins to scoop out a depression in the beach, large enough to accommodate her entire body – loose sand flying in all directions as the flippers scoop and slap, back and forth. The task completed, the reptile rests for a moment. Now her hind flippers go into action, the left and right sides alternately scooping a precisely shaped 30-cm-deep cavity in the firm moist sand. This egg cavity completed, the turtle proceeds to lay in it approximately one hundred moist and glistening white eggs, the shape and size of ping-pong balls. She breathes deeply all the while and tears roll from her eyes as special glands keep them moist.

Once her eggs are laid, the turtle covers her nest with sand, flicking it haphazardly over the place to camouflage it. Then, without a backward glance, she ploughs her way down the beach and makes her way through the breakers to sea. To watch the whole performance is to experience a flashback to the great age of reptiles when dinosaurs roamed the earth.

The turtle will return to the same beach several times in one nesting season in order to lay further nests, and nothing short of death will deter her powerful instincts. Often turtles that come ashore to lay have horrible shark bites, or a missing flipper, yet they struggle on regardless. Research by the Natal Parks Board is uncovering new knowledge about our marine turtles; each year many are marked with numbered tags while nesting. It seems that after nesting, a turtle disappears for two to three years before returning, travelling great distances across the surface of the oceans in the interim.

The young turtles hatch in about two months, leaving the nest simultaneously and heading straight for the sea (127). Mortality is high among them; they fall prey to birds, ghost crabs, jackals and oil pollution. Dogs dig up the eggs, and adults are killed for food in great numbers along the coasts to the north of South Africa. Turtles usually return to nest on the beach where they were born, which probably explains the steady increase in the numbers nesting along Natal beaches, where they are protected by law.

Cape gannets (128) spend their lives at sea searching for and diving among shoals of fish, coming ashore only to breed on small islands such as the one inshore off Lamberts Bay along the west coast.

Cape cormorants (129) are a memorable feature of South Africa's south and west coasts, flying single-file like a living necklace as they move low across the ocean searching for fish shoals. They too nest on islands off the coast.

Although the Cape fur seal (130) might come ashore on a quiet beach, or during a storm at sea, they prefer the safety of offshore islands such as Seal Island in False Bay. These large marine carnivores feed on fish, for which they can dive to a depth of 50 metres and remain submerged for several minutes. The Cape fur seal produces a single youngster each year and in former times there were numerous large breeding colonies on the mainland, such as along the Robberg promontory at Plettenberg Bay. If seals are clumsy on land, they more than compensate for this by the sheer grace with which they move in the water, often frolicking in the waves for the sheer fun of it.